The Story of
Musical
Organizations

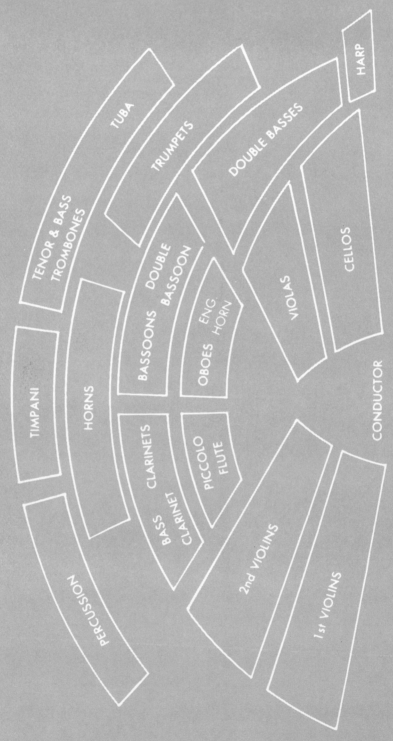

The Sections of the Orchestra

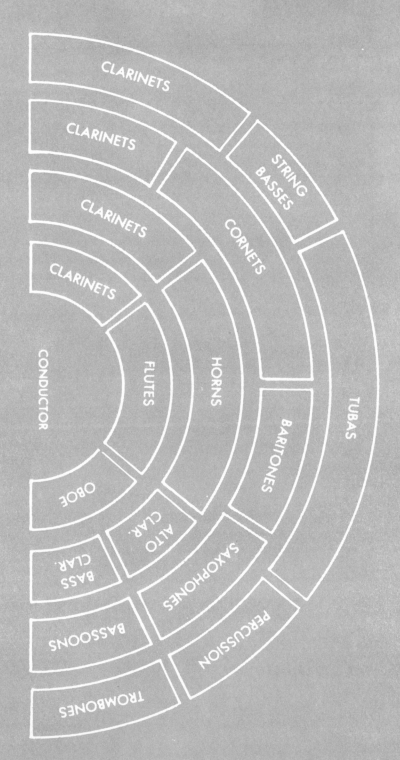

The Sections of the Band

The Story of
Musical
Organizations

By ROBERT W. SURPLUS

Illustrated by GEORGE OVERLIE

Musical Books for Young People

LERNER PUBLICATIONS COMPANY
MINNEAPOLIS, MINNESOTA

To Amy and Melanie

International Copyright Secured. Printed in U.S.A.

Library of Congress Catalog Card Number: 62-20805

Third Printing 1964
Fourth Printing 1966

CONTENTS

Do You Know the Organizations in a Music Department?

The night of the big concert in any school is a time of great excitement. The pupils who are members of the orchestra, band, chorus, and dance band perform for their parents and friends. Often, small groups of musicians perform in addition to the big organizations.

Today, most schools have large music departments. Often, there are several choruses, plus instrumental groups. One chorus is for girls, one for boys, and one for both girls and boys. One instrumental group uses stringed instruments, while another has no stringed instruments.

Do you know all about the different organizations in a music department? How are bands different from orchestras? Which started first—bands, orchestras, or choruses? How many kinds of choruses are there? Why are there several kinds of choruses? These are some of the questions that people ask about musical organizations.

The answers to these questions are found in the pages of this book. As you read on, you will find many interesting facts about the musical organizations in your own home town.

Choral Music
Early Choral Music

The first choral music was chanted. Many centuries ago when man made his first simple instruments, he used them to accompany chants. These chants were full of rhythm and had very little melody or tune. Early man used these chants to accompany his dances.

Many years later when the church had become the center of music, chanting was still used. The chants of the early church were far different from those used with early man's dancing. They were religious and, of course, more serious.

In chanting, the words were sung to very much the same rhythm as they were spoken. There were stopping or breathing places, the same as when people speak. Everyone sang the same part. Musicians call this kind of music *monophony* (mo-NAHF-o-nee), or "one-voice" music.

After a while, people who wrote music began to write more than one part. Their first attempts at writing more than one part sound strange to our ears. We say that they wrote the second part an *interval* of a *fifth* below the first part. An interval is the distance between two notes. When there is an interval of a fifth, the distance between the notes is five steps. Here is an example of the way *America* looks written in fifths.

6

Have someone play this on the piano for you, or try it yourself. The sound is rather empty and hollow, isn't it? Yet, singers sang this way once.

Sometimes musicians sang in fourths. Fourths also have an empty, hollow sound. Here is *America* in fourths.

Notice that in both these examples, the notes of the lower part move in exactly the same way as the notes of the upper part. The next step that composers took was to allow the second part to go in a different direction than the first part. Soon, musicians started writing the kind of music we know as *polyphony* (po-LIF-o-nee), or "many-voiced" music.

At first, polyphony had three parts. Each part was different from the other—the notes were different and the time they were held was different. Soon, musicians were writing music in four parts, then five, then six. Choral music began to grow more difficult to sing. It got to the point where there were as many as fifty different parts being sung at one time. The remarkable thing was that they sounded good together.

Polyphony is something like the rounds you sang in school. Remember that in a round each part started at a different time, and that the music sounded good when all the parts were being sung together. Rounds are not written out to show how they look when all the parts are being sung. If they were, the music would look quite a lot like polyphony did. Here is a familiar song written as a three-part round. Notice how the music looks when all three parts are being sung.

ARE YOU SLEEPING ?

In the round shown here, all the voices are equally important. Such was not the case in much earlier choral music. Finally, musicians began to treat all the voices the same, and the parts were arranged like they are today. The names *superius, altus, tenor,* and *bassus* were given to the parts. Can you see how close these names are to *soprano, alto, tenor,* and *bass,*—the names we use for the different parts today?

In time, polyphonic music began to change. Little by little, **writing** of music in chords began to appear. The style of writing a choral accompaniment to a melody became more and more popular. Finally, polyphony gave way to *homophonic* (homo-FAHN-ic) music. This kind of music has a single melody with a chord background. In choral music, the melody is usually found in the soprano part. The other parts sing notes of chords that sound well with the soprano part. Here is *Are You Sleeping* written in this style. Notice how different this is from the example of a three-part round.

The choirs of today sing music of all kinds. Sometimes they sing polyphonic music. At other times, a program will be made up of music from the present. Choral directors are always looking for good music, old or new, to put on their programs.

Different Kinds of Choruses

There are several kinds of *choruses,* the name musicians give to groups which sing music. We have different kinds of choruses because different voices are used, or people of different ages are singing.

The kind of a chorus that is found in a grade school is a *treble chorus.* This means that the music that is sung is written in treble clef. Sometimes, everyone will sing the same part. We call this *unison* singing.

Twinkle, Twinkle, Little Star

At other times they sing two parts.

Musicians call two-part treble music SA music. The S stands for soprano and the A for alto. Three part music is called SSA music. In SSA music the chorus is divided into three parts — first soprano, second soprano, and alto. If boys and girls of elementary school age sing SSA music, it must be specially arranged to fit the notes their voices can sing. Musicians say that it must fit the *range* of their voices.

First Soprano

Twin - kle, twin - kle, lit - tle star, How I won - der what you are.

Second Soprano

Twin - kle, twin - kle, lit - tle star, How I won - der what you are.

Alto

Twin - kle, twin - kle, lit - tle star, How I won - der what you are.

A girls' chorus or a women's chorus will also sing SSA music. Since the music is for older people, it is usually harder than music for grade school choruses. Also, the range of the parts will be different. Older voices can go higher and lower than the voices of people of grade-school age. Sometimes, a women's chorus will sing music that is SSAA—two soprano and two alto parts.

A men's chorus or glee club will sing TTB or TTBB music. T stands for *tenor,* the higher of the men's parts, and B stands for *bass,* the lower of the parts. When there are two tenor parts, the higher part is called *first tenor,* and the lower *second tenor.* The melody is usually found in the second tenor part. The same thing happens to

11

the bass part—the higher bass part is called *first bass,* and the lower part *second bass.* Here is what TTBB music looks like. Notice that the tenor part is written in treble clef. The men's voices are not really this high—they sound an *octave* or eight notes lower than the part is written.

There are several kinds of *mixed choruses.* A mixed chorus is a chorus with both boys and girls or men and women in it. It is possible to have a mixed chorus that sings SSA music. In such a chorus the boys' voices would not have changed. This means that their voices have not started to lower into men's voices yet.

Most boys' voices start to change in junior high school. Some start sooner than others. Within one class it is possible to have boys whose voices haven't started to change, boys whose voices are changing, and boys whose voices have changed.

12

There are special arrangements of music for boys whose voices are changing. Also, when arrangements are made for junior high choruses, the parts do not as a rule call for all the notes in the range of a voice. Usually, the arranger writes those notes that sound best for each type of voice.

Sometimes, there are mixed choruses that sing three parts. They are called SAB choruses since the music is written for soprano, alto, and bass voices. Such choruses are formed when there are no good tenors to be found, or when there are only a few men or boy singers to be had. Music of this kind is very often used in junior high schools. The bass part in a lot of SAB music does not go as low as most bass parts. It is often written especially so that young basses can sing the notes.

People in high school and adults sing SATB music — music for soprano, alto, tenor, and bass voices. SATB music looks like the example below.

Twinkle, Twinkle, Little Star

Sometimes the composer will write the parts so there are two soprano notes or two bass notes. In such a case, half of the sopranos will sing one note and half the other note. The basses will do the same. Sometimes, the composer will write SSAATTBB music. Other composers have written music that calls for a chorus to be divided into two separate parts—two choruses in one. Such music is usually quite hard, and a good chorus is needed to sing it.

14

We have been using letters to show the voice parts that are used in choral organizations. Here is a group of letters that tell about another kind of singing. Do you have any idea what SPEBSQSA means? Well, these are the initials of a very active organization—the *Society for the Preservation and Encouragement of Barber-Shop Quartet Singing in America.* This organization has national meetings at which quartets from all over America sing. There are even glee clubs which sing in barbershop style.

What is barber-shop style? It is a type of singing that first became popular around 1900. Four men usually make up a quartet, although there are lady barber-shop singers, too. The men sing the following parts: first tenor, second tenor, baritone, and bass. The second tenor sings the tune, and the first tenor sings a high part above the tune. The bass singer usually has a deep voice that sounds well on low notes, and the baritone supplies the notes that are needed to fill in the harmony. Quite often, barber-shoppers sing "echo" type arrangements. In such arrangements, the second tenor starts off and is answered by the other three voices. *Sweet Adeline* is a favorite song of barber-shop singers.

Small groups of only a few people often sing together. There are girls' trios (three singers), mixed quartets (four singers), sextets (six singers), octets (eight singers), and other groups. In many schools, a small group of the very best singers is given a special name. Whenever music is needed, such special groups are often called upon to sing.

The Orchestra

The Sections of the Orchestra

An orchestra is a musical organization made up of string, woodwind, brass, and percussion instruments. Musicians say that these different instruments make up the *sections* of the orchestra. Sometimes the different sections are called *choirs.* When a musician talks about the *brass choir,* he is talking about all the brass instruments in the orchestra. When he talks about the *string choir,* he is talking about all the strings in the orchestra.

The most important section of the orchestra is the *string section.* The string section is made up of violins, violas, cellos, and bass violins. The violins are divided into two parts—first violin and second violin.

The *woodwind section* consists of flutes, oboes, clarinets, and bassoons. Orchestra music also calls for the piccolo, English horn, bass clarinet, contra-bassoon, and saxophone.

The *brass section* includes trumpets, French horn, trombones, and tuba.

The most important members of the *percussion section* are the timpani, the snare drum, the bass drum, and the cymbals. Percussion players are called upon to play many other instruments, such as the triangle, castanets, xylophone (ZI-lo-fone), glockenspiel (GLOCK-en-schpeel), and celesta (che -LES-ta).

The Early Orchestra

Early orchestras were not at all like the orchestras of today. They were called *accidental orchestras.* No one knew just what instruments there would be when it came time to play. As you can imagine, the sound of these very early orchestras was not always the best.

For years choral music had been more important than instrumental music. People have always had voices to use in singing, but good instruments to play were not always found. Because it took a long time for men to develop good instruments, choral music was for years far more popular than instrumental music.

Around 1600, in the city of Florence, Italy, a new kind of music was started. This new music was called *opera*. It used singing and acting to tell a story. Singing was still far more important than playing an instrument, but opera did need an orchestra to play an *accompaniment*.

Opera proved to be very popular. It was also a great help to instrumental music. Instead of just a harpsichord, a few lutes (a plucked string instrument), violins, and bass viols, the orchestra began to grow larger.

A composer called Claudio Monteverdi helped with this. When he wrote his opera, *Orfeo,* he asked for an orchestra that was huge for those times. While he thought of the strings as the most important part, he also wanted *balance* between all the instruments. He didn't want one group of instruments to be stronger than another.

The strings were the most important section in the early orchestras. This was because the string instruments were made before most woodwind or brass instruments. The woodwinds and brasses were quite crude when compared with the strings. In fact, many of the other instruments had not even been invented when some of the very best string instruments ever made were being produced.

Composers wrote for the instruments that were handy. Since the strings were ready for use, it was only natural to write music for them. Composers knew what to expect from the strings, but they couldn't always be sure how the early wind instruments would sound. The string sound became the important sound in the early orchestra, and it has always remained so.

For a long time, composers did not write out all the parts as they do today. They wrote the *melody,* or tune, and the *bass,* or lowest part. Sometimes they wrote another part or two, but often they gave only an outline. The musicians made up their own parts from a *figured bass.*

Here is an example of figured bass. The melody is in the upper line. The bass part is found on the lower line. The numbers under the bass part are the figures that told the musicians what notes to play.

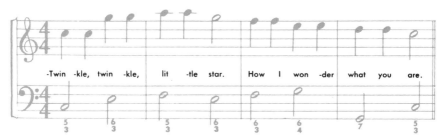

This is how figured bass was read. The musician looked at the bass part and called each bass note one. Then he looked at the numbers written below each note. Starting with one, he counted up the number of notes that the figures told him to count. He then played these notes as part of the music.

The next example shows the easiest way to do this. Numbers have been marked after the notes of the first three chords to help you with the counting.

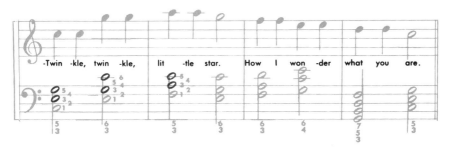

The strings and oboes or flutes usually played the melody, while the *harpsichord* filled in the missing notes—the notes called for by the numbers of the figured bass. The harpsichord was a keyboard instrument, very much like the piano. The conductors of the early orchestras were the harpsichord players. The instruments all grouped around the harpsichord, so they could follow the conductor's lead.

The Start of the Modern Orchestra

The figured bass lasted for quite a long time, but finally composers stopped using this way of writing music. Instead, they wrote out every part they wanted played. This caused a great improvement in the sound of the orchestra. Musicians were no longer free to make up their own parts. They had to play exactly what was on the page.

There were other reasons why orchestras began to sound better. As we mentioned earlier, the strings were ahead of the other instruments. They were developed first, and composers wrote for the instruments they had at hand. However, instrument makers were becoming more interested in some of the other instruments. As other instruments were improved, and as new ones were invented they were added to the orchestra. Clarinets, for example, made their way into the orchestra between 1750 and 1800.

Musicians themselves were anxious to improve the orchestra. They knew that if they improved their own playing the whole orchestra would sound better, so they worked hard at becoming better players.

Good conductors were also hard at work. They worked for balance. They didn't want one section of the orchestra to play so loud that another section couldn't be heard. They were also working for good ensemble (on-SAHM-bul) playing—all the musicians playing exactly together.

Three groups of people then were hard at work trying to build better orchestras—the instrument makers, the musicians, and the conductors.

The composer, Franz Joseph Haydn (1732-1809), is given much of the credit for starting the modern orchestra. When he stopped writing figured bass parts for the harpsichord, he had to use some other instrument or instruments to fill in the missing notes. Haydn gave this job to the wind instruments. Up to this time, the wind instruments had not been very important. Haydn made them grow in importance. Not only did they fill in the missing notes, but they were also given the melody at times. They were starting to take the same place in the orchestra that they have today.

In the music that he wrote late in his life, Haydn called for an orchestra very much like that of today. True, it was smaller than present-day orchestras and there were fewer of some of the instruments, but Haydn's ideas influenced others and helped get ready for larger orchestras. He wrote parts for the following instruments:

violins	two clarinets
violas	two bassoons
cellos	two horns
bass violins	two trumpets
two flutes	timpani
two oboes	

Sometimes he also wrote parts for the trombone and contra-bassoon.

The size of orchestras was not the same as today. The real early orchestras were large if they had twenty players. Between 1700 and 1750 the average size varied between twenty and forty players. By Haydn's time, the size was between thirty to fifty players.

The orchestra at the court of Mannheim, Germany was one of the best of its day. The famous composer, Mozart (1756-1791), heard this orchestra play in 1777. He was very excited about how it sounded and wrote home to his father:

> "The orchestra is very good and powerful, on each side ten or eleven violins, four violas, two oboes, two flutes, two clarinets, two horns, four violin-cellos (cellos), four fagotti (bassoons), four contra-bassi (bass violins), trumpets, and timpani. You wouldn't believe what a glorious effect a symphony makes when played with flutes, oboes, and clarinets. Oh, if we only had clarinets!"

Mozart was to make sure that his music had clarinets! Listen to his wonderful *G Minor Symphony* and his *Clarinet Concerto* to hear how well he wrote music for the clarinet.

We mentioned that three groups were helping to build better orchestras—the musicians, the instrument makers, and the conductors. As you have read on, have you thought of another group of people who were making changes in orchestras?

Some of the great composers wrote for an orchestra that did not exist. That is, they wrote for more instruments than were found in the orchestras of their day. You have already read how Haydn changed the orchestra when he wrote interesting parts for the wind instruments to play. Mozart helped when he wrote *chromatic* parts (music with a lot of sharps and flats, or music that used the chromatic scale.)

The orchestra of Haydn and Mozart was not always powerful enough for the music of Beethoven (1770-1827). He wanted a greater variety of sounds in his music. Although the trombone had been used before in opera and church music, Beethoven used it in a symphony. Instead of two horns, he wrote music for three or four horns. He also gave the timpani much more important parts to play. He liked a big string section, and he called for the violins to play higher than they had before.

The composer, Berlioz (1803-69), influenced orchestra music a lot. He asked for sounds that other composers never dreamed of. He even wanted the strings to play *col legno* (coe LEN-yo). This means that the string players turn the bow so that the wooden part of the bow can be bounced off the strings. He also liked to use *muted* brasses. To mute brasses, a device that looks something like an ice cream cone is put in the open end, or *bell*. He quite often wrote for *stopped* horns. To stop a horn, the hand is placed far up the bell. This makes the horn sound differently than usual. It also changes the pitch of the horn. Berlioz also thought of new ways of playing percussion instruments—hitting a cymbal with a timpani stick was a good example. Many of his ideas about writing music for the orchestra were put into a book about *orchestration* (the art of writing music for an orchestra). Even today, this book is studied by young composers.

Other important changes were taking place. Around 1815 valves were invented for horns and trumpets. Up to this time, horn and trumpet parts were mainly "bugle call notes". When valves were invented, these instruments were able to play chromatic scales (scales using all the sharps and flats).

The woodwind instruments were also improved. They had always been very hard to play in tune. The new woodwinds were not only easier to blow, but also easier to play in tune. The bass clarinet was invented during this time.

The German composer, Wagner (1813-83), was happy about the improvement in instruments. He wrote music for a very large orchestra. A lot of his music called for fifteen woodwinds, twenty-one brass instruments, harp, percussion, sixteen first violins, sixteen second violins, twelve violas, twelve cellos, and eight bass violins. This was over one hundred instruments. Quite a lot different from the early orchestras!

The Orchestra Today

During the last days of the 19th century and the early years of this century, composers were writing music for large orchestras, much like that of Wagner's. Later in this century, some composers wrote music for small orchestras, very much the same size as the orchestras of Mozart's and Haydn's time. Other composers write for very large orchestras, and they use a lot of percussion instruments.

24

The size of a major symphony orchestra today is around one hundred players. Conductors change the size of the orchestra to suit the kind of music the orchestra is playing. If more instruments are needed than are usually used, *extras,* or musicians who are not regular orchestra members, play.

How the orchestra sits on the stage is up to the conductor. Here is a chart showing how many orchestras are seated.

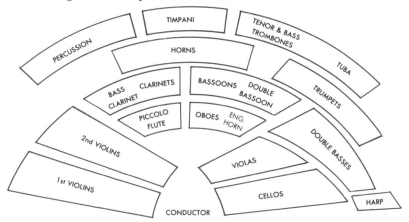

Not all orchestras will have the players seated in the same way. Sometimes the trumpets and trombones are placed on the other side, near where the percussion is shown in this chart. Some conductors move the horns more to the left. Others put the trumpets back of the horns. Sometimes the second violins are placed to the right of the conductor—where the cellos are in this picture. Then, the cellos are seated where the second violins are in this picture.

In most junior and senior high schools and in many grade schools, there are orchestras. Many times these orchestras will not follow the seating plan shown. There are a number of reasons for this. They may not have enough instruments to follow this plan. One section may not be as strong as desired, and the conductor may change the seating. If the seating in your orchestra is different from this chart, your conductor has a good reason for the difference.

The Band
The Sections of the Band

A band is a musical organization made up of woodwind, brass and percussion instruments. Usually, bands do not use stringed instruments. That is how they are different from orchestras. However, there are some exceptions to this rule. Very often a bass violin is used in the band, and the Air Force Band even uses four cellos. But, those few stringed instruments that are used are not as important as the other instruments. A band does not need stringed instruments to sound like a band, while an orchestra must have strings to sound like an orchestra.

The Band in Europe

The band is descended from early groups of fifes, drums, and trumpets that were part of the armies of Europe. These early bands were used to give signals to the soldiers, as well as to give the beat for marching.

In parts of Europe, especially Germany and Austria, there were early town bands. The players in these bands worked for the towns. At first, their job was to sound the hours of the day from towers in which they kept watch. When it came time to signal that an hour had gone by, they made musical sounds.

In time, their duties changed. They also began playing for town and state events, and even at weddings. They learned popular music for outdoors, marches for town events, and accompaniments for group singing.

The instruments on which these towermen played were *trombones* and *cornetts*. The cornetts were wooden instruments with a mouthpiece like today's cornet. They were not like the cornet in any other way. Instead of having valves, they had finger holes very much like those of a recorder, one of the ancestors of the flute.

When you read about the orchestra, you discovered that the stringed instruments were developed before the wind instruments. At the time of these early bands, it was easy to tune the strings. Large numbers of stringed instruments were used to play together.

The wind instruments could not be tuned very well. At a time when the orchestra was growing larger, the wind bands stayed small. This was because of the tuning problem. If a large number of wind instruments had been played together, the sound would not have been very good.

Can you imagine a band of two oboes, two clarinets, two bassoons, and two horns? Sometimes two flutes, a *serpent* and drums were also used. This was the kind of band that the army of Frederick the Great listened to. By the way, the serpent mentioned above was a bass cornett. It was a large wooden instrument with six finger holes. The name serpent was given to the instrument, because it was curved like a snake so the player could cover the finger holes.

By the end of the eighteenth century, public band concerts outdoors were heard in all the capital cities of Europe. The idea came from the earlier tower musicians who played popular outdoor music. Also, the German Army bands played a few pieces of music each night before retreat. The people enjoyed the music, and the custom soon spread to France and other countries.

In 1825 between thirty and forty players were found in many bands in Europe. By 1850 some bands had around fifty musicians, and by 1867 when an international band contest took place in Paris, one band had eighty-five musicians. Although it got a later start, the band began to grow in size the same as the orchestra had. Although some instruments have since been added and some dropped, the band at the end of the nineteenth century was quite a lot like the band of today.

American Bands

There were bands in New York and Boston very early in our history. These bands played marches for patriotic events in the early days of American Independence.

One of the early bands that has lasted until today is the famous United States Marine Band. This band was first started in 1798. In 1800, the instruments used were two oboes, two clarinets, two horns, and a drum. The band grew in size and by 1899 it had sixty players.

The man who started the *concert band* in the United States was Patrick Gilmore. A concert band is a band that gives concerts. It is different from the older *military bands* that played mostly marches. Gilmore was a fine cornet player. In those days good cornet players usually became *bandmasters,* or directors. Gilmore liked to organize huge festivals with thousands of singers accompanied by a great big band. He was the first person to make the band popular in the United States.

John Philip Sousa was the most famous bandmaster this country has ever known. In 1880 he was named director of the United States Marine Band, and he conducted this famous organization with great success. In 1892 he left the Marine Band and formed his own band. This band traveled all over the United States giving concerts. Sousa's Band toured Europe five times, and even made one trip around the world. Probably no other musical group was better known and more loved by the American people than the Sousa Band.

Because Sousa wrote such snappy marches he was named "The March King". Listen to *Washington Post, El Capitan,* and *Semper Fidelis* to hear some of his fine marches. Also, make sure that you hear *The Stars and Stripes Forever,* the most famous march Sousa wrote.

The Goldman Band in New York City is another famous band. It was first organized in 1911 by Edwin Franko Goldman. In 1918 the band started giving free outdoor concerts at Columbia University. Later, the concerts were changed to Central Park and Prospect Park. Dr. Goldman had a lot of influence on bands and band music. Not only did he write a lot of music for the band, but he also encouraged others to do the same.

The Goldman Band concerts are still heard on summer evenings in New York City. Today, Richard Franko Goldman, the son of the founder, is the conductor. If you are ever in New York City, go to hear one of these free concerts. A Goldman Band concert in Central Park is a thrilling experience!

There have been other famous bands and bandmasters in this country. Cities like Allentown, Reading, and York, Pennsylvania, and Hagerstown, Maryland, and Fort Dodge, Iowa have been noted for their fine bands. During the summer months, you can hear concerts in many cities and towns across the land. Today, some of the best bands are found in high schools and colleges. Even grade schools and junior high schools have very good bands.

The Marching Band

Can you remember the last time you saw and heard a good marching band? Maybe you were at a parade, or perhaps at a football game. The peppy music, the fine marching, and the flashy uniforms all go together to give a lot of enjoyment.

The marching band of today is much different from the bands of your parents' younger days. While there are still some bands that do just regular military marching, the high school and college bands do all sorts of tricky marching. Besides marching at parades, they give "shows" at football games.

Band shows are planned well ahead of time. Often, the show is planned around one main idea. The band director knows he has so many minutes for the show. First, he picks an idea for the show, and then he decides what formations the band will make. The next step is to pick the music for each part of the show. Sometimes he uses music the band already knows. Many times, the music must be specially arranged.

When the music has been put together for the show, it is handed out to the members. The band then learns how to play it. Next, they walk through the formations that will be used in the show. Finally, they put the music and marching together. The smooth performance seen at the football game takes hours of work.

Often, band directors put on shows that are built around fancy marching. Many directors teach the band members to take eight steps to every five yards. This makes it possible to do a lot of drills that look very hard to those watching. The people are amazed when the rows always end up on a white yard line at the end of the music. They don't stop to think how carefully the director counted the number of steps the marchers take and the number of beats in the music.

Most bands use a marching plan something like the one shown. Notice where the different instruments are. The trombones are usually up front, followed by the other brass instruments. The drums are in the middle where all the members can easily hear the beat, and the woodwinds are back of the drums. Most marching bands have a drum major or majorette, and many also march with a group of baton twirlers.

The Concert Band

The concert band and the orchestra have the same purpose. Both organizations perform music for the enjoyment of audiences.

The band has always borrowed a lot of music from the orchestra. Of course, the music had to be arranged so the band could play it. The clarinets in a band often play the same parts that the violins do in the orchestra. The arranger must *transpose* (write in another key) these parts to make them sound right for the clarinet. Most of the parts for the other band instruments are changed, too. Although more and more music is being written for the band, it still borrows from the orchestra.

Besides music borrowed from the orchestra, a concert band will include many other kinds of music. To many people, hearing a band play a march is the high point of a concert. Light and entertaining pieces of music are usually found on the program, also. Cornet solos are as popular today as ever. Most band concerts will feature some kind of soloist. Band directors try to put music on programs that will appeal to their audiences.

The concert band is different from the marching band. Most band directors will use fewer brass and percussion instruments in a concert band than in a marching band. They want the marching band to have a big, full sound for outdoors. For the concert band, they are interested in a quieter and better-balanced sound.

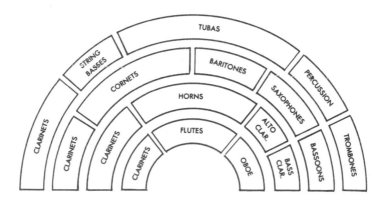

The seating plan of a concert band is much different from the way a marching band lines up. Here is the seating plan of a large concert band. In the marching band, the brass instruments are found in the front. In the concert band, the woodwind instruments are placed in the front. Compare this chart with the seating plan of the orchestra. Notice how the woodwinds sit in almost the same place in the band as the strings do in the orchestra.

Small Ensembles

There are many small groups of instruments that can be played together. They are of different sizes. Here is a list of some of them and the number of people who play in them.

NAME	NUMBER OF PLAYERS
Trio	3
Quartet	4
Quintet	5
Sextet	6
Septet	7
Octet	8
Nonet	9

These small groups, or *ensembles,* sometimes include a piano. They may be all wind instruments, or they may be all string instruments. They can also include both strings and wind instruments. Music has been written for all sorts of combinations.

Music for small groups used to be called *chamber music*. This meant that such music sounded good in a drawing room of a person of wealth.

The string quartet was always a favorite of those who liked this kind of music. It is interesting to know that the parts played in a string quartet are the same as those played by the strings of an orchestra: first violin, second violin, viola, and cello.

In our schools we often find small ensembles. Clarinet quartets seem to be a favorite. They can be made up of four B♭ clarinets, or two B♭ clarinets, an alto clarinet, and a bass clarinet. Woodwind groups using all the woodwinds are also used.

We find many trumpet trios. People always seem to enjoy hearing a trumpet trio. There are other brass ensembles such as brass quartets made up of two trumpets, a french horn and a trombone, or a french horn quartet, or a brass sextet—two trumpets, a french horn, a trombone, a baritone, and a bass horn.

Playing in a small group is different from playing in a band or orchestra. There is only one player to each part. This means that each player must be very dependable. The player must play very carefully for every note he plays is easily heard. He must be able to play no louder or softer than the rest of the ensemble, for usually perfect balance is desired. Ensemble playing requires fine musicians.

The Dance Band
The Four Sections

The dance band consists of a group of musicians usually numbering between seven and seventeen. Like the orchestra and band, it is made up of sections. A dance band usually has four sections.

The *saxophone section* has three to five players. If there are three saxes, the parts are first alto sax, second tenor sax, and third alto sax. If a band is large enough to have four saxes, the fourth part would be a fourth tenor part. Many large bands have five saxophones. The fifth part is played by the baritone sax.

Usually, the musicians in the sax section *double,* that is, they play more than one instrument. Sax players usually double on clarinet. However, many sax players play other reed instruments, such as flute, oboe, bass clarinet, or bassoon. They usually double on reed instruments, but there have been exceptions. Jimmy Dorsey, who had a fine dance band that your parents will remember, played saxophone, but he was a fine cornet player too.

The size of the *trumpet section* also varies according to the size of the band. A very small dance band might have only one trumpet. Musicians usually are happier when there are two or three. Fuller harmony is played when there are two or three in the section. Four trumpets is usually the largest number in the trumpet section, although some very large bands have had five.

The number of trombones also varies according to the size of the band. Usually, from one to four will be the number in the *trombone section.*

The fourth section of the dance band is the *rhythm section.* The rhythm section consists of piano, drums, bass fiddle (dance band talk for bass violin) and guitar. Again there is no set rule as to the number of instruments. Piano and drums are always necessary, and the bass fiddle helps a lot. The guitar is usually the last instrument to be added.

Some dance bands have a fifth section. They use stringed instruments, too—violins, violas, and cellos. Dance bands with strings are not seen as often as those with only four sections.

Many dance bands have one or two *vocalists,* or singers. If the singer is a girl, she rarely plays an instrument in the band. But, if the singer is a man, he often plays in the band and sings as well. Some dance bands have singing groups—a *quartet* (four singers), or even larger groups.

36

It Started in New Orleans

The dance band really got its start many years ago in the city of New Orleans. New Orleans was different from most cities in this country. It had been French and Spanish before it became part of the United States.

New Orleans was a musical city. There was a fine opera house and good orchestras and bands. The people heard many kinds of music. Those who didn't have the money to attend concerts made their own music.

The Negroes were the poor people of New Orleans. Most of them made a very poor living. They lived in their own sections of the city. They may not have had a lot, but they had one thing that proved to be very important—a love for music.

They sang at work—in the fields, at the docks, and in the warehouses. They made musical instruments out of anything they could get their hands on. When they could get real instruments, they formed their own bands.

The Negroes played the music they heard, but they played differently than the white musicians. Most of them couldn't read a note of music, so they had to play "by ear". Many times they *improvised,* or made up music, as they went along. Of course their playing was influenced by the things they knew—their African background, the white music of New Orleans, and the French and Spanish music, too.

In time, the music they played was called *jazz.* Nobody really seems to be sure just how this name started. It may have been called something else, because for a while it was spelled j-a-s-s instead of j-a-z-z.

The earliest jazz bands came from the brass bands the Negroes organized. These bands were mainly marching bands, but they did other things besides marching. There used to be an interesting custom in New Orleans. People who wanted to advertise something hired a band. Then the band would be hauled around in a wagon, playing as they rode through the city. Of course, they attracted attention. Sometimes, two band wagons would meet at a corner. Then they would hold a contest to see which band could outplay the other.

In the early days of jazz, sidewheel steamers paddled up and down the Mississippi river. Many had their own bands. Soon, this kind of music spread to other cities—Memphis, St. Louis, Kansas City. Finally, it even reached Chicago. White musicians also began to play this music. Jazz was here to stay!

Arranged Music

The early jazz musicians did not read music. Jazz was played by a small group of musicians who usually knew each other quite well. They knew what to expect of each others playing, and they used their ears to make the parts sound good together.

During the 1920's this kind of playing started to change. There were several reasons why. First, records were very popular. People listened to them, and they also danced to them. Records were all the same length. The leader had to know just how long to play if the band's music was to fit on a record. When radio started, there was even more need for carefully timed music. Also, some band leaders felt that they could interest more people in dance music if the music was played more smoothly and quietly than the music of the earlier jazz bands.

Arrangers, musicians who wrote out the parts for the other men, were hired to arrange music for dance bands. Many big bands were formed to play this arranged music. During the 1930's and 1940's the music they played was called *swing.* Swing was really arranged jazz.

The 1930's and 1940's were the big years for dance bands. Your parents probably danced to the music of some of the big bands of those days. Some of the most famous names were: Benny Goodman, Glenn Miller, Artie Shaw, Charlie Barnet, Tommy Dorsey, Jimmy Dorsey, Count Basie, Duke Ellington, Woody Herman, and Harry James.

The dance bands that are found in our junior and senior high schools are models of these famous bands of the past.

The Dance Band's Music

During the days when the big dance bands were most popular, each band had its own style and own sound. The arranger was the person largely responsible for this.

Many bands could not afford to spend the money to pay an arranger. Arrangements called *stocks* were published for such bands. Anyone could buy them—they were not special. Stocks were written to sell to as many bands as possible. They were arranged in such a way that they would sound good with small dance bands or large ones.

Dance band arrangements usually start off with a solid-sounding introduction. After the introduction (shortened to *intro* by musicians), one of the sections will play the melody. Sometimes the brass section will play a few short notes called *figures* when the saxes are holding a long note. Or, one section will softly play chord tones while another section plays the melody. At other times, one section will play a *riff* as a background to the melody. A riff is a phrase, or musical idea, that is repeated over and over. Here is an example of a riff.

Medium Bounce

When dance bands used arranged music, playing by ear was seldom done. There was one exception to this. In arranged music, one soloist is often given a chance to *improvise,* or make up music, as he goes along. The other musicians play background music, while the soloist makes up a part built around the melody. A musician who can improvise well is called a good *ride man.*

Combos

A combo is a small group of musicians who play for listening or dancing. There is no rule about what instruments you will find in a combo. One combo had a tenor sax, piano, drums, bass fiddle, and guitar. Another one consisted of trumpet, trombone, clarinet, piano, and drums. A third combo used an accordion, drums, tenor sax, vibraphone, and bass fiddle.

Combos are popular today for two reasons. The first reason is that they cost far less to run than big bands. Record companies have found it is much cheaper to pay for a combo than a large band. Of course, combos have played for years in many places where a big band would be too noisy or too expensive.

The second reason for the popularity of combos is the type of music that is recorded today. Many of the records made since about 1955 have been *rock 'n roll,* or a variation of this style. Rock 'n roll is a style of playing that puts great importance on a rhythmic accompaniment. The second and fourth beats of every measure are often *accented* (played louder). Many rock 'n roll pieces use a *triplet* over and over. A triplet occurs when three notes are evenly played on one beat. Here are some common rock 'n roll rhythm patterns.

While many young people seem to like this style of music, those who have heard the other kind of dance band music recognize a big difference. The big dance bands needed better musicians and more practice to play their kind of music.

People Need Music

You have learned some things about musical organizations. You have found out that there are many ways in which the different organizations are alike, and you have also discovered some differences. You know something of their past, as well as their present.

Now that you have finished this book, will you think about two things? Why have these organizations developed? Why does music exist?

The answer to both questions is simple. Music and musical organizations exist because over the centuries people have had a need for them. There is no other reason. People need music to make life more enjoyable. But music needs people, too—to perform it and listen to it.

Think about your future in music. If you are not already a member, join one of your school music organizations tomorrow. People need music!

ABOUT THE AUTHOR

Robert W. Surplus, a native of Gouldsboro, Pennsylvania, has been active in music education almost twenty years. He has had experience in every phase of music education in the public schools, and has taught all age levels from kindergarten through graduate school. Formerly Supervisor of Music at Red Lion, Pennsylvania, Associate Professor at Shippensburg State College, Shippensburg, Pennsylvania, and Instructor at Teachers College, Columbia University, he is at present, an Assistant Professor in the College of Education, University of Minnesota. A graduate of Susquehanna University with a Bachelor of Science degree, and of Teachers College, Columbia with a Master of Arts degree, he is presently completing the requirements for a doctorate at Columbia University.

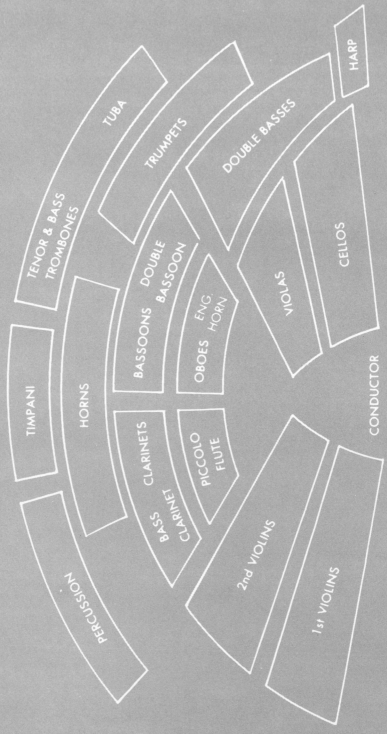

The Sections of the Orchestra